I Am a Child of God

{ A Year of Prepared Family Night Lessons
and Activities to Strengthen Your Home }

I Am a Child of God

{ A Year of Prepared Family Night Lessons and Activities to Strengthen Your Home }

Kimiko Christensen Hammari

CFI
An imprint of Cedar Fort, Inc.
Springville, Utah

ISBN: 978-1-4621-2092-5

Library of Congress Control Number: 2017914967

Published by CFI, an imprint of Cedar Fort, Inc.
2373 W. 700 S., Springville, UT, 84663
Distributed by Cedar Fort, Inc., cedarfort.com

Cover design by Shawnda T. Craig
Cover design © 2017 Cedar Fort, Inc.
Edited by Heather Holm

Printed in the United States of America

10 9 8 7 6 5 4 3 2 1

Printed on acid-free paper

For Heather

for always

believing

in me

CONTENTS

July

August

September

October

November

December

HOW TO USE THIS BOOK

This book provides a year's worth of family home evening lessons. In order to get the most out of this manual and reinforce what your children are learning in Primary, teach the lessons in order. The lessons are divided into monthly themes and subdivided into weekly themes. Four lessons are provided for most months. However, in some months, there are only three. In those cases, use the extra week to review what you learned previously. Each lesson is divided into the following sections:

Resources

Scriptures, Primary songs, hymns, and pictures from the *Gospel Art Book*. (Note: The *Gospel Art Book* is available at lds.org. You can download and print pictures, or show the pictures to your children on a computer or another electronic device. You can order a copy of the *Gospel Art Book* at store.lds.org.)

Lesson

A brief explanation of the theme is given with corresponding scriptures and discussion questions.

Activity

The activities are meant to reinforce what is taught in the lesson, so they may not be the games your family is used to playing. Many lessons include separate activities for younger children and older children. Generally, the activities for younger children are for ages three to seven, and those activities for older children, eight to eleven. However, don't use this guideline as a firm rule. Some younger children may be advanced for their age, and some older children may still enjoy the activities for younger children.

Challenge

These challenges should be completed during the week before the next Monday. At the beginning of each family home evening, follow up with your children on the previous week's challenge. Discuss their successes and help them with any problems or concerns.

Activity Printouts

You can download and print the activities at primaryhelper.com/downloads.

JANUARY

I Am a Child of God,
and He Has a Plan for Me

"The Spirit itself beareth witness with our
spirit, that we are the children of God"
(Romans 8:16).

God is my Heavenly Father. He knows and loves me.

RESOURCES

(Select one from each category.)

Children's Songbook
I Am a Child of God (2)
My Heavenly Father Loves Me (228)

Hymn
O My Father (292)
I Know My Father Lives (302)

Scriptures
Psalm 82:6
Galatians 4:7

Lesson

Did you know that we have two fathers? We have a father here on earth, who is the father of our bodies. We also have a Heavenly Father. He is the father of our spirits. We lived with Him before we came to earth. Even though we are no longer with Him, He still knows and loves us, just as our earthly father does. Heavenly Father knows our names, our talents, our likes and dislikes, our strengths and weaknesses, and everything else about us. He knows what happens to us during the day and cares if we are happy or sad.

In the scriptures we can read about Heavenly Father appearing to different prophets. He called them by name, showing that He knew them. When Heavenly Father and Jesus Christ appeared to Joseph Smith in the Sacred Grove, the first thing Heavenly Father did was call Joseph by name.

It is comforting to know that we have a loving Heavenly Father who cares about us. Even though we cannot see Him, we can pray to Him anytime, anywhere. He will always listen and answer our prayers in ways that will help us make it back to Him.

Read and discuss Jeremiah 1:5.
What did the Lord mean when He told Jeremiah that He knew him before he was formed in the belly?
What do you think Heavenly Father knew about you before you were born?

Activity

Younger Children: Color the picture on page 12. You can download and print the activity at primaryhelper.com/downloads.

Older Children: See page 5. You can download and print the activity at primary-helper.com/downloads.

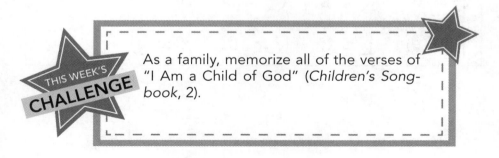

THIS WEEK'S CHALLENGE

As a family, memorize all of the verses of "I Am a Child of God" (*Children's Songbook*, 2).

SECRET CODE

Using the code, decode the message on the next page. *Solution on page 137.*

A = 😊	G = 😈	M = 😟	S = 😵	Y = 😣
B = 😠	H = 😕	N = 😤	T = 😆	Z = 😟
C = 😏	I = 🤓	O = 😎	U = 😈	
D = 😲	J = 😩	P = 😮	V = 😏	
E = 😃	K = 😀	Q = 😠	W = 😐	
F = 😟	L = 😃	R = 😋	X = 😲	

WEEKS 2&3

Heavenly Father's plan is a plan of happiness.

RESOURCES

(Select one from each category.)

Children's Songbook
He Sent His Son (34)
I Will Follow God's Plan (164)

Hymn
Come, Follow Me (116)
I Believe in Christ (134)

Scriptures
Acts 4:12
1 John 1:2

Gospel Art Book
Jesus Christ (1)
The Lord Created All Things (2)

Lesson

We lived with Heavenly Father before we were born. He wanted us to become like Him and have all the things that He has. One day He presented a beautiful plan to us. Under this plan, we would come to earth to receive a physical body like His. We would also have families and choose between right and wrong. We call this plan the plan of happiness, because if we follow it, we will find great joy.

We are here on earth because we chose to follow Heavenly Father's plan. If we live righteously, we will return to live with Heavenly Father after we die. But we won't always make the right choices. Sometimes we will sin. Because Heavenly Father loves us, He provided a way for us to repent and be forgiven. Through the Atonement of Jesus Christ, we can become clean from sin and return to live with Heavenly Father someday.

Read and discuss John 3:16.
Who is Heavenly Father's only begotten son?
Why is Jesus Christ the center of Heavenly Father's plan of happiness?

Activity

All Ages: Play the game on pages 8 and 9. You can download and print the activity at primaryhelper.com/downloads. The instructions are below.

Materials

1 dice
1 pawn for each player (You can use beans, coins, small pieces of candy, or any small objects that fit on the board.)

Rules

1. Take turns rolling the dice, in order of age from youngest to oldest, to see how many spaces to move your pawn.
2. If you land on a space with a dot, draw a card and follow the instructions.
3. The person to reach the finish line first wins.

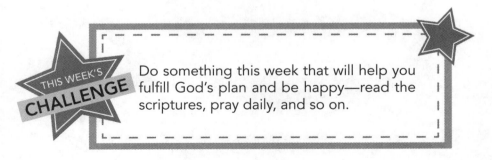

THIS WEEK'S CHALLENGE

Do something this week that will help you fulfill God's plan and be happy—read the scriptures, pray daily, and so on.

You were reverent during Primary. *Move ahead one space.*	You helped a boy at school who was sad. *Move ahead two spaces.*	You helped your parents make dinner. *Move ahead one space.*
You helped your neighbor rake leaves. *Move ahead one space.*	You read a book to your little sister. *Move ahead three spaces.*	You said your bedtime prayers. *Move ahead one space.*
You paid your tithing. *Move ahead one space.*	You read the scriptures. *Move ahead two spaces.*	You told a lie. *Go back one space.*
You didn't listen to your parents. *Go back one space.*	You weren't reverent in Primary. *Go back two spaces.*	You stole a pack of gum. *Go back one space.*
You went to a movie instead of to church. *Go back three spaces.*	You hit your brother. *Go back one space.*	You called someone a bad name. *Go back two spaces.*

WEEK 4

I have agency, and I am responsible for my choices.

Lesson

Agency is one of the greatest gifts Heavenly Father has given us. Having agency means having the freedom to make choices for ourselves. No one can force us to do anything against our will.

Before we came to earth, there was a great war in heaven. When Heavenly Father presented the plan of happiness, He told us that we would need to make good choices in order to return to Him. But Heavenly Father knew it would not be easy and that we would need a savior. Lucifer said that he would be our savior and force us to keep the commandments so we could return to Heavenly Father. That was not a good plan, because we wouldn't have the freedom to choose. Jesus Christ said He would be our savior and teach us the right way. Then we would each decide which path to take. Heavenly Father was very pleased with this plan, and so were we. We chose to come to earth and follow Jesus Christ.

RESOURCES

(Select one from each category.)

Children's Songbook
Nephi's Courage (120)
Dare to Do Right (158)

Hymn
Choose the Right (239)
Teach Me to Walk in the Light (304)

Scriptures
D&C 101:78
Articles of Faith 1:2

Gospel Art Book
Adam and Eve Teaching Their Children (5)
Family Prayer (112)

Here on earth we are faced with choices each day. We have the freedom to choose between right and wrong, and we will be responsible for our choices. If we choose the right, we will be blessed. If we choose to sin, we will have to suffer the consequences.

Read and discuss Helaman 14:29–31.
What happens if we make good choices?
What happens if we choose evil?

Activity

All Ages, Option 1: Color the picture "Jesus Christ created the earth as a place where I can learn to choose the right" in the January 2012 *Friend* magazine, available at lds.org/friend/2012/01/coloring-page?lang=eng.

All Ages, Option 2: Play the game from last week's lesson (see pages 8 and 9). Discuss how we have to take responsibility for our choices. When a player picks a card that says he made a bad choice and has to go back a space or two, liken it to taking responsibility for our choices and repenting. Discuss how making good choices helps us move forward on the path to Heavenly Father.

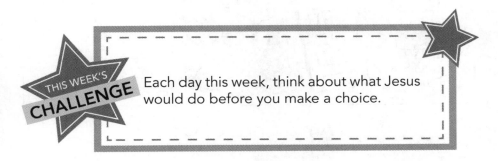

THIS WEEK'S CHALLENGE

Each day this week, think about what Jesus would do before you make a choice.

I Am a Child of God

FEBRUARY

The Earth Was Created for Heavenly Father's Children

"We will make an earth whereon these may dwell; and we will prove them herewith, to see if they will do all things whatsoever the Lord their God shall command them" (Abraham 3:24–25).

WEEK 1

Jesus Christ created the earth under the direction of Heavenly Father.

RESOURCES

(Select one from each category.)

Children's Songbook
My Heavenly Father Loves Me (228)
All Things Bright and Beautiful (231)

Hymn
All Creatures of Our God and King (62)
For the Beauty of the Earth (92)

Scriptures
Colossians 1:16
John 1:10

Gospel Art Book
The Lord Created All Things (2)
The Earth (3)

Lesson

As part of the plan of happiness, we needed a place where we could receive a physical body and be tested. Jesus Christ created the earth under the direction of Heavenly Father. We are here on earth to learn and grow and take care of our physical bodies.

Jesus Christ created many wonderful things for us to enjoy here on earth. Let's read about the creation of the earth in Genesis chapter 1.

Read and discuss Genesis 1.
What did Jesus create first? Last?
Why did He rest on the seventh day?

Activity

Younger Children: Print the puzzle on page 16. Cut out the pieces, and then see if you can put the puzzle back together. You can download and print the activity at primaryhelper.com/downloads.

Older Children: See page 17. You can download and print the activity at primary-helper.com/downloads.

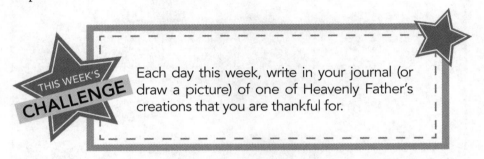

THIS WEEK'S CHALLENGE

Each day this week, write in your journal (or draw a picture) of one of Heavenly Father's creations that you are thankful for.

Jesus Created the Earth for Us

Find seven differences in the two pictures below. *Solution on page 137.*

WEEK 2

The Fall was part of God's plan.

Lesson

God gave Adam and Eve two important commandments. One was to multiply and replenish the earth (have children). The other was not to eat from the tree of knowledge of good and evil. If they did, they would have to leave the Garden of Eden.

One day, Satan came to Eve and told her to eat the fruit from the tree of knowledge of good and evil. She said she would not. She did not want to break the commandment. Satan convinced Eve that it was the right thing to do. It would make her wise and help her to have children, which was another commandment she wanted to keep. Eve ate the fruit and told Adam that he should too. He realized she was right and ate the fruit. They had to leave the Garden of Eden. This event is known as the Fall of Adam, or the Fall.

When Adam and Eve left the Garden of Eden, they learned what it was like to work. They

RESOURCES

(Select one from each category.)

Children's Songbook
The Second Article of Faith (122b)
Stand for the Right (159)

Hymn
How Gentle God's Commands (125)
How Great the Wisdom and the Love (195)

Scriptures
1 Corinthians 15:22
Mosiah 3:19

Gospel Art Book
Adam and Eve Kneeling at an Altar (4)
Adam and Eve Teaching Their Children (5)

also understood the difference between good and evil and sorrow and happiness. However, one really important thing happened. They were able to keep the commandment to have a family. Because of this, they had much joy and were able to grow spiritually.

Many people view the Fall as a bad thing. But it is actually part of God's plan. If Adam and Eve had remained in the Garden of Eden, they wouldn't have known good from evil. They wouldn't have been able to have children. And they wouldn't have been able to practice their agency, or freedom to choose.

Read and discuss 2 Nephi 2:25.
What does it mean that "Adam fell that men might be"?
How did the Fall bring about joy?

Activity

Younger Children: Draw a picture of what you think the Garden of Eden looked like.
Older Children: See page 26. You can download and print the activity at primary-helper.com/downloads.

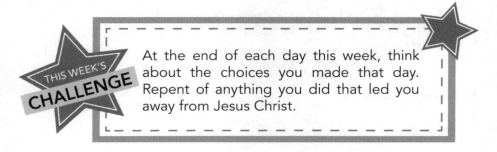

THIS WEEK'S CHALLENGE

At the end of each day this week, think about the choices you made that day. Repent of anything you did that led you away from Jesus Christ.

WEEK 3

I have been sent to the earth to gain a body and be tested.

Lesson

Did you know that Heavenly Father has a body just like ours? Some people believe He is a spirit, but we learn in the Doctrine and Covenants that God has a body of flesh and bone: "The Father has a body of flesh and bones as tangible as man's; the Son also" (130:22). Heavenly Father wanted us to have a body like His so that we could become more like Him. That is one of the reasons we came to earth.

Another purpose of this life is to be tested. Heavenly Father wants us to choose between good and evil. In the premortal life, we chose to follow Jesus Christ. Now we must prove that we will. If we keep the commandments and repent when we sin, we can live with Heavenly Father again.

RESOURCES

(Select one from each category.)

Children's Songbook
I'm Trying to Be like Jesus (78)
Choose the Right Way (160)

Hymn
Do What Is Right (237)
Know This, That Every Soul Is Free (240)

Scriptures
Ether 3:19
Moses 6:9

Gospel Art Book
The Earth (3)

Read and discuss Abraham 3:22–25.
What is the purpose of life?
How does God test us?

Activity

Younger Children: God has made all of our bodies unique. We may look different, but we are all God's children and are here on earth for the same purpose. Play a matching game with the pictures of the children on page 22. Print two copies of the cards, cut them out, turn them face down on a table, and see who can get the most matches. You can download and print the activity at pimaryhelper.com/downloads.
Older Children: Do the word search on page 23. You can download and print the activity at pimaryhelper.com/downloads.

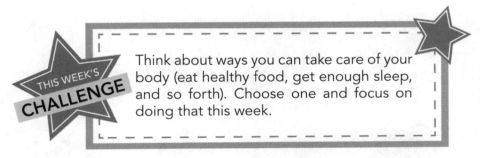

THIS WEEK'S CHALLENGE

Think about ways you can take care of your body (eat healthy food, get enough sleep, and so forth). Choose one and focus on doing that this week.

WORD SEARCH

Below is an excerpt from the Old Testament (Genesis 1:26–27). Find the words in bold in the word search. Remember, words may appear forward, backward, horizontally, vertically, or diagonally. *Solution on page 137.*

Eve and Adam

R	C	S	N	G	E	D	B	Q	C	L	P
O	A	C	E	B	D	M	Q	G	G	G	Q
H	T	Z	J	U	A	F	O	W	L	Y	J
J	T	Q	F	I	S	H	B	J	D	E	B
Y	L	I	H	D	O	M	I	N	I	O	N
Q	E	Q	E	A	R	T	H	K	E	Y	Z
O	C	R	E	E	P	I	N	G	F	D	E
Y	W	L	P	L	I	K	N	E	S	S	G
H	A	W	E	E	I	M	A	G	E	E	V
M	C	K	N	S	K	I	Z	F	N	O	T
Y	K	V	U	O	U	Q	J	A	K	M	Q
F	E	M	A	L	E	O	M	N	B	T	F

And God said, Let us make **man** in our **image**, after our **likeness**: and let them have **dominion** over thee **fish** of the sea, and over the **fowl** of the air, and over the **cattle**, and over all the **earth**, and over every **creeping** thing that creepeth upon the earth.
So God created man in his own image, in the image of God created he him; **male** and **female** created he them.

WEEK 4

If I keep the commandments, I can live with Heavenly Father again.

Lesson

Heavenly Father loves us very much and wants us to live with Him forever. He told Moses, "For behold, this is my work and my glory—to bring to pass the immortality and eternal life of man" (Moses 1:39). That means He will do anything to help us return to Him.

Heavenly Father has also told us that we need to be free of sin in order to return to Him. We must keep the commandments. In 1 Nephi 10:21 we learn that "no unclean thing can dwell with God." Fortunately Heavenly Father understands that life isn't easy and that we all make mistakes. We can repent when we sin. But we need to try our best each day to choose the right. If we keep the commandments, we will return to live with Heavenly Father after we die and receive great joy.

RESOURCES

(Select one from each category.)

Children's Songbook
Keep the Commandments (146)
Teach Me to Walk in the Light (177)

Hymn
Guide Me to Thee (101)
I'll Go Where You Want Me to Go (270)

Scriptures
Proverbs 4:4
Jarom 1:9

Gospel Art Book
City of Zion Is Taken Up (6)
The Sermon on the Mount (39)

Read and discuss John 14:15.
Why will we keep the commandments if we love God?
How can we show our love to Heavenly Father?

Activity

All Ages: Play a game of Simon Says. Tell your children that they will receive a small treat or reward at the end if they do their best to obey all of Simon's instructions. Liken this to the blessings we receive for keeping the commandments.

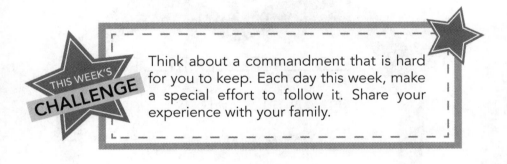

THIS WEEK'S CHALLENGE

Think about a commandment that is hard for you to keep. Each day this week, make a special effort to follow it. Share your experience with your family.

MISSING VOWELS

Below is a verse from the Book of Mormon. Fill in
the missing vowels to read a message about the Fall.
Solution on page 137.

A A A A A A A A
E E E E E
I I   O

_D _M F_LL TH_T

M_N M_GHT B_;

_ND M_N _R_,

TH_T TH_Y

M_GHT H_VE J_Y.

(2 N_PHI 2:25)

MARCH

Jesus Christ Is Our Savior

"Hearken ye to these words. Behold, I
am Jesus Christ, the Savior of the world"
(D&C 43:34).

WEEK 1

Jesus Christ taught the gospel and set an example for us.

Lesson

Jesus Christ lived a perfect life. He obeyed the commandments with exactness and never gave into temptation. He loved Heavenly Father and wanted to do His will. Jesus is often called the light of the world because He set a perfect example for us and has shown us the way back to Heavenly Father.

One day Jesus went to John the Baptist and asked to be baptized. John was surprised because he didn't think Jesus needed to be baptized. Jesus didn't have any sins. In the Book of Mormon, Nephi explains that Jesus was baptized to show "unto the children of men that, according to the flesh he humbleth himself before the Father, and witnesseth unto the Father that he would be obedient unto him in keeping his commandments" (2 Nephi 31:6–7). It is just one of the many examples of how Jesus showed us the way to keep the commandments.

Read and discuss John 8:12.
How is Jesus the light of the world?
How do we walk in darkness if we don't follow Him?

Activity

Younger Children: Do the dot-to-dot on page 30 and then color the picture. Discuss ways that Jesus is the light of the world. You can download and print the activity at primaryhelper.com/downloads.

Older Children: Complete the activity on page 31. Then discuss ways that Jesus is the light of the world. You can download and print the activity at primaryhelper.com/downloads.

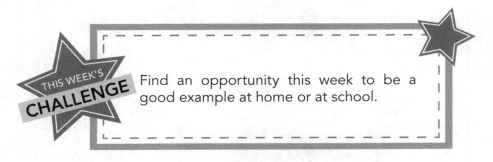

THIS WEEK'S CHALLENGE

Find an opportunity this week to be a good example at home or at school.

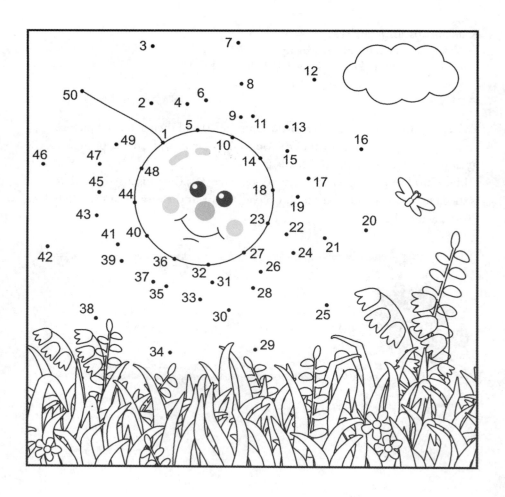

Find the two suns that are the same. Think about how Jesus is the light of the world and how He has brought joy into your life. *Solution on page 137.*

WEEK 2

Because of Christ's Atonement, I can repent and live with God again.

Lesson

When Heavenly Father sent us here to earth, He told us that we could only return to Him if we kept the commandments. But He also knew that life would be hard and we would sin. He loves us so much that He provided a Savior for us. Jesus Christ died for us so that we can live with Heavenly Father again. It is called the Atonement.

There are three parts to the Atonement. First, Jesus suffered in the Garden of Gethsemane. He paid the price of our sins so that we won't have to if we repent. Next He died on the cross, giving Himself as a sacrifice for all mankind. His body was placed to rest in a tomb. On the third day, He was resurrected. His spirit and body were reunited. He is alive again and will never be able to die again.

Because of Christ's great gift to us, we will all be resurrected someday. But more important, we

RESOURCES

(Select one from each category.)

Children's Songbook
He Sent His Son (34)
He Died That We Might Live Again (65)

Hymn
Cast Thy Burden upon the Lord (110)
How Great the Wisdom and the Love (195)

Scriptures
Alma 34:8
D&C 18:11

Gospel Art Book
Jesus Praying in Gethsemane (56)
The Crucifixion (57)

can repent and be cleansed from our sins. The Atonement of Jesus Christ makes it possible to live with Heavenly Father again.

Read and discuss Helaman 5:9.
How did Jesus Christ redeem the world?
Why is He the only way back to our Heavenly Father?

Activity

All Ages: For this activity you will need a dry erase board, a permanent marker, and a dry erase marker. First, write the word *sin* on the dry erase board with the permanent marker. Show your children that you can't erase it. Tell them that sometimes we feel that way about our sins. Sometimes we fear that they are permanent. Using the dry erase marker, cover the word *sin* and then erase it. The board will be clean! Liken this to the Atonement and explain that we cannot become clean from sin on our own. We need Jesus Christ to help us.

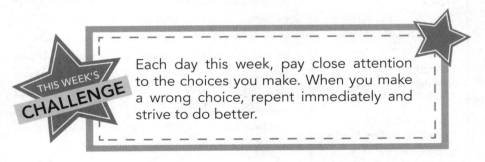

THIS WEEK'S CHALLENGE

Each day this week, pay close attention to the choices you make. When you make a wrong choice, repent immediately and strive to do better.

WEEK 3

Because Jesus Christ was resurrected, I will be too.

RESOURCES

(Select one from each category.)

Children's Songbook
Did Jesus Really Live Again? (64)
Jesus Has Risen (70)

Hymn
That Easter Morn (198)
Christ the Lord Is Risen Today (200)

Scriptures
Mormon 7:5
Alma 40:23

Gospel Art Book
Mary and the Resurrected Jesus Christ (59)
Jesus Shows His Wounds (60)

Lesson

After Jesus Christ died on the cross for us, His body was placed in a tomb. On the third day, when His disciples went to check on Him, they found His tomb empty. Jesus had overcome death and had been resurrected. His spirit and His body were reunited.

Through the Atonement of Jesus Christ, we too will be resurrected. Our spirits and our bodies will come together again and will be perfected. We will no longer suffer illness or injury. For example, a blind man will be able to see again. A deaf man will hear again. Someone who lost a leg in this life will be able to walk and run perfectly. Resurrection is a gift to everyone on this earth because Heavenly Father and Jesus love us so much.

Read and discuss Mosiah 16:6–9.
How is death "swallowed up in Christ"?
Why does "the grave hath no victory"?

Activity

All Ages: Make resurrection rolls (see page 140 for the recipe).

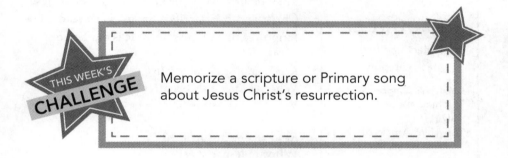

THIS WEEK'S CHALLENGE

Memorize a scripture or Primary song about Jesus Christ's resurrection.

WEEK 4

Jesus Christ is our Savior.

Lesson

This month we've been learning about Jesus Christ and His sacrifice for us. Let's read a few scriptures that discuss how He is our Savior.

Read and discuss John 3:16.
Who is God's only begotten son?
What is everlasting life?

Read and discuss John 10:15.
Who are Jesus's sheep?
Why did Jesus lay down His life for them?

Read and discuss Doctrine and Covenants 18:11.
What did Christ suffer for us?
What does He want all men to do?

Activity

All Ages: Watch a video about the Savior at lds.org/biblevideos.

RESOURCES

(Select one from each category.)

Children's Songbook
To Think about Jesus (71)
The Third Article of Faith (123)

Hymn
Our Savior's Love (113)
I Know That My Redeemer Lives (136)

Scriptures
Matthew 1:21
1 John 2:2

Gospel Art Book
Jesus Carrying a Lost Lamb (64)
Jesus at the Door (65)

THIS WEEK'S CHALLENGE

Find an opportunity this week to bear your testimony of Jesus Christ or to be a good example.

APRIL

Jesus Christ Restored His
Church in the Latter Days

"I have sent forth the fulness of my gospel
by the hand of my servant Joseph"

(D&C 35:17).

WEEK 1

After Jesus Christ and His Apostles died, gospel truths were lost.

RESOURCES

(Select one from each category.)

Children's Songbook
The Chapel Doors (156)
When I Go to Church (157)

Hymn
Awake and Arise (8)
The Day Dawn Is Breaking (52)

Scriptures
Isaiah 60:2
Matthew 24:24

Gospel Art Book
The Ascension of Jesus (62)

Lesson

When Jesus Christ was on the earth, He established His Church. He called Apostles to help Him and gave them the priesthood authority, or the power to act in His name. Because the Apostles held the priesthood, they were still able to lead the Church after Jesus died.

Unfortunately, the Apostles faced much persecution. Many people didn't believe in their teachings and treated them badly. Eventually all of the Apostles were killed and nobody else had the priesthood power. The Church of Jesus Christ was no longer on the earth.

For centuries, men lived in darkness because they did not have the fulness of the gospel. People still lived good lives and believed in Jesus Christ, but the true Church of Jesus Christ was no longer on the earth. A special prophet would be called to restore the gospel.

Read and discuss Amos 8:11.
What is a famine?
What does the famine in this verse symbolize?

Activity

All Ages: Turn off all the lights in the room and shut the blinds and curtains. Ask one of your children to read a scripture. When he says that he can't see it, explain that just as the room is dark, people lived in darkness when the true Church was taken from the earth. Turn on the lights and ask the child again to read the scripture. Explain that the lights are like the fulness of the gospel, which gives us the power to see things clearly.

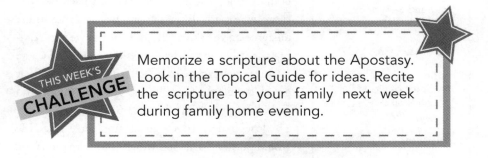

THIS WEEK'S CHALLENGE

Memorize a scripture about the Apostasy. Look in the Topical Guide for ideas. Recite the scripture to your family next week during family home evening.

WEEK 2

Heavenly Father and Jesus Christ appeared to Joseph Smith.

RESOURCES

(Select one from each category.)

Children's Songbook
This Is My Beloved Son (76)
The Sacred Grove (87)

Hymn
The Spirit of God (2)
Joseph Smith's First Prayer (26)

Scriptures
Malachi 3:1
2 Nephi 3:11

Gospel Art Book
Joseph Smith Seeks Wisdom in the Bible (89)
The First Vision (90)

Lesson

In the spring of 1820, Joseph Smith was fourteen years old. He and his family were searching for a church to join. Joseph was very confused because there were many different churches, and they didn't all agree on the same things. One day he was reading the Bible and came across the following verse: "If any of you lack wisdom, let him ask of God, that giveth to all men liberally, and upbraideth not; and it shall be given him" (James 1:5).

Joseph decided to do as this verse said. He would pray and ask God which church to join. One morning he went into a grove of trees and knelt down to pray. He had faith that God would answer him, but something very unexpected happened. In the Pearl of Great Price, he described his experience: "I saw a pillar of light exactly over my head, above the brightness of the sun, which descended gradually until it fell upon me. . . . When the light rested upon me I saw two Personages, whose brightness and glory defy all description, standing above me in the air. One of them spake unto me, calling me by name and said, pointing to the other— This is My Beloved Son. Hear Him!" (JS—H 1:16).

Heavenly Father and Jesus Christ instructed Joseph not to join any of the churches. Even though all of the churches taught good things, none of them were the true Church of Jesus Christ. When Jesus and the Apostles died, the true Church was taken from the earth. Joseph learned that he had a sacred mission to fulfill. He would be the prophet of the Restoration and restore the true Church of Jesus Christ on the earth.

Activity

All Ages: Watch *Joseph Smith: The Prophet of the Restoration* (available at lds.org). If you don't have time to watch the entire video, watch the segment on the First Vision.

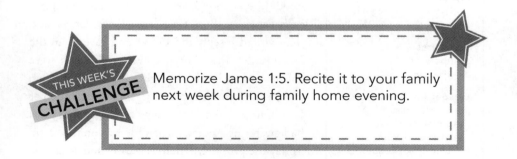

THIS WEEK'S CHALLENGE

Memorize James 1:5. Recite it to your family next week during family home evening.

WEEK 3

Priesthood authority was restored by heavenly messengers.

Lesson

Last week we learned that Joseph Smith was called to be the prophet of the Restoration. He could not restore the Church of Jesus Christ without the priesthood. Because no one on the earth had the priesthood, he received it from heavenly messengers.

John the Baptist visited Joseph Smith and Oliver Cowdery and gave them the Aaronic Priesthood. Joseph and Oliver were then able to baptize each other. A short time later, Peter, James, and John visited Joseph and Oliver and gave them the Melchizedek Priesthood. Oliver and Joseph were able to give each other the gift of the Holy Ghost, and Joseph was then able to organize the Church of Jesus Christ. He held the same authority that Jesus had given His Apostles when He was on the earth. Today the prophet, Thomas S. Monson, leads the Church with the same priesthood authority.

Read and discuss Joseph Smith—History 1:67–72.
From whom did Joseph Smith and Oliver Cowdery receive the Aaronic Priesthood?
From whom did they receive the Melchizedek Priesthood?

Activity

All Ages: Look through Church magazines such as the *Friend* and find five pictures of things that we have because of the priesthood (temples, scriptures, and so on).

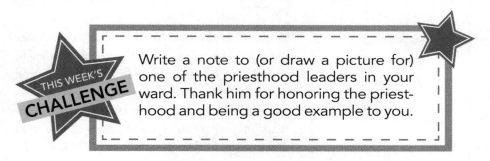

THIS WEEK'S CHALLENGE

Write a note to (or draw a picture for) one of the priesthood leaders in your ward. Thank him for honoring the priesthood and being a good example to you.

WEEK 4

Joseph Smith translated the Book of Mormon and restored gospel truths.

RESOURCES

(Select one from each category.)

Children's Songbook
The Golden Plates (86b)
Book of Mormon Stories (118)

Hymn
The Iron Rod (274)
As I Search the Holy Scriptures (277)

Scriptures
2 Nephi 33:10
D&C 17:6

Gospel Art Book
Moroni Appears to Joseph Smith in His Room (91)
Joseph Smith Translating the Book of Mormon (92)

Lesson

One of Joseph's Smiths duties was to translate the gold plates, a record of the people in ancient America. Jesus had visited these people and established His Church among them, just as He did with the people in the Bible. After several years of preparation, Joseph received the gold plates at the Hill Cumorah. Joseph did not know the language the gold plates were written in, but that did not matter. He also received the Urim and Thummim, which helped him translate the sacred record. With the help of God, Joseph was able to complete the translation.

The Book of Mormon does not replace the Bible. In fact, they go hand in hand to teach us the fulness of the gospel. When the Bible was translated, many precious truths were lost. The Book of Mormon contains the missing truths.

Read and discuss the sixth paragraph of the Introduction to the Book of Mormon.
What did Joseph Smith say about the Book of Mormon?
Why is it the most correct of any book on earth?

Activity

Younger Children: Draw a picture of your favorite Book of Mormon prophet.
Older Children: Do the word puzzle on page 48. You can download and print the activity at primaryhelper.com/downloads.

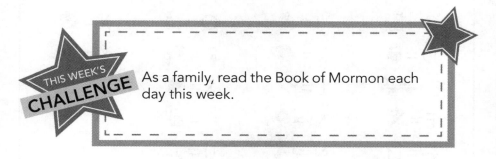

THIS WEEK'S CHALLENGE

As a family, read the Book of Mormon each day this week.

SECRET CODE

Using the key below, decode the message on the following page This activity will give you an idea of what Joseph Smith went through when he translated the Book of Mormon. *Solution on page 137.*

A = 🖌	H = 🏀	O = 🎓	V = 📕
B = ᴬᴮC	I = ✂	P = 📜	W = ⚗
C = 📚	J = 🎒	Q = 🔬	X = 🎨
D = 🍎	K = 📙	R = 📚	Y = ✏
E = 🚌	L = 📎	S = 🖼	Z = 🏛
F = 📐	M = 🌐	T = 🧮	
G = 📝	N = 📖	U = ♫	

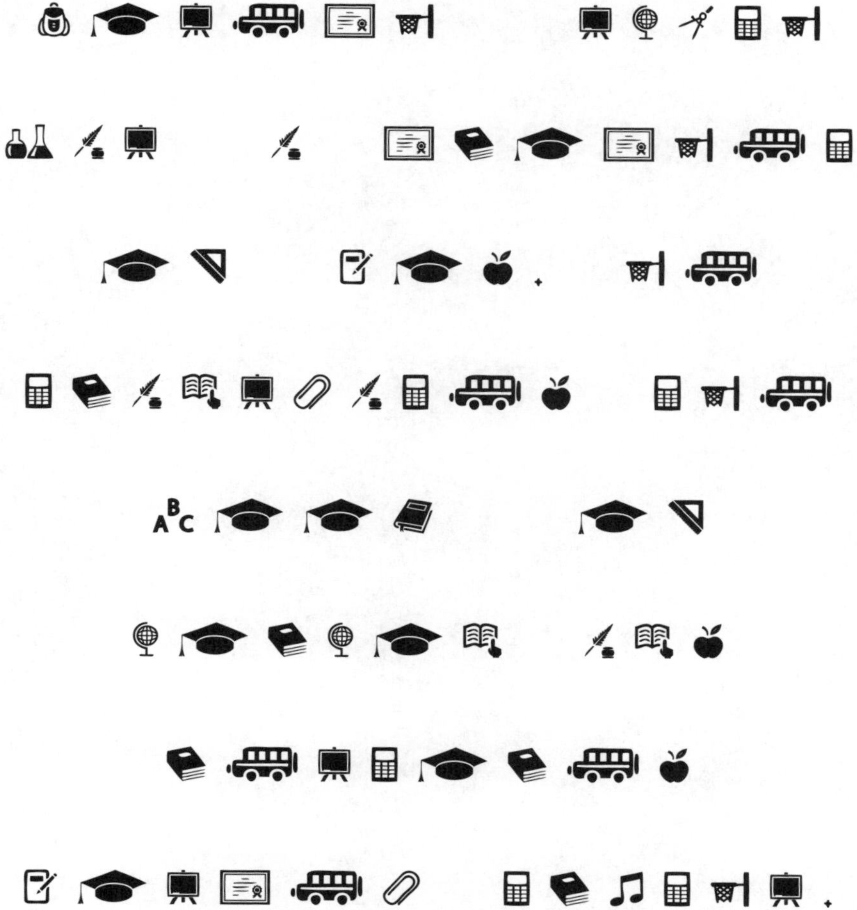

MAY

Prophets Teach Us to Live the Restored Gospel

"Surely the Lord God will do nothing, but he revealeth his secret unto his servants the prophets" (Amos 3:7).

WEEKS 1&2

The living prophet leads the Church under the direction of Jesus Christ.

RESOURCES

(Select one from each category.)

Children's Songbook
Follow the Prophet (110)
Latter-day Prophets (134)

Hymn
We Thank Thee, O God, for a Prophet (19)
Come, Listen to a Prophet's Voice (21)

Scriptures
Ephesians 4:11
D&C 43:3

Gospel Art Book
Thomas S. Monson (137)

Lesson

Jesus Christ is the head of the Church. But He is not here on the earth to lead us like He was in New Testament times. Instead, He leads the Church through the living prophets. President Thomas S. Monson and his Apostles receive revelation from Jesus Christ on how to lead the Church.

In Doctrine and Covenants 1:38 we read, "What I the Lord have spoken, I have spoken, and I excuse not myself . . . whether by mine own voice or the voice of my servants, it is the same." When the prophet speaks through the power of the Holy Ghost, he is speaking for Jesus Christ. We should treat his words as seriously as we would if Jesus Christ said them to us.

The prophet and Apostles teach us about Jesus Christ and explain the scriptures to us.

Sometimes they give us new commandments. When this happens, we should remember that they are speaking for Jesus Christ.

Read and discuss Doctrine and Covenants 21:5.
How should we receive the words of the prophet?
For whom does the prophet speak?

Activity

All Ages: Watch videos from the "Meet the Apostles" series at lds.org/children/videos/apostles?lang=eng. Discuss what you have learned about these great men.

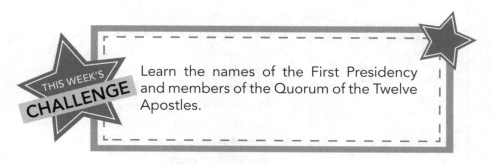

THIS WEEK'S CHALLENGE

Learn the names of the First Presidency and members of the Quorum of the Twelve Apostles.

WEEK 3

Prophets teach me to pay tithing.

RESOURCES

(Select one from each category.)

Children's Songbook
I'm Glad to Pay a
  Tithing (150a)
I Want to Give the Lord
  My Tenth (150b)

Hymn
We Give Thee But Thine
  Own (218)
Because I Have Been
  Given Much (219)

Scriptures
D&C 64:23
D&C 119:4

Gospel Art Book
Payment of Tithing (113)
A Tithe Is a Tenth Part
  (114)

Lesson

In 1838 Joseph Smith received a revelation that we must pay tithing. The word *tithing* means "one-tenth," and the law of tithing states that we must give one-tenth of all we earn to the Lord. Tithing money is used to help pay for church buildings, temples, and other things that we need in order to perform God's work here on earth.

Sometimes we are tempted not to pay our tithing. It can be easy to want to use the money for something we want very much. But we must remember that everything we have comes from God. He is not asking much by requiring that we return one-tenth of our earnings. We will receive great blessings if we keep the law of tithing. Let's read about some of those blessings in the scriptures.

Read and discuss Malachi 3:8–10.

What are some of the blessings Malachi said we would receive for paying tithing?

What are some of the blessings you have seen in your own life because you paid tithing?

Activity

All Ages: The Lord said that if we pay our tithing, He will open the windows of heaven and pour out blessings. Print out the picture of the window on page 60. Draw pictures (or write a list) of some of the blessings your family has received for paying tithing. You can download and print the activity at primaryhelper.com/downloads.

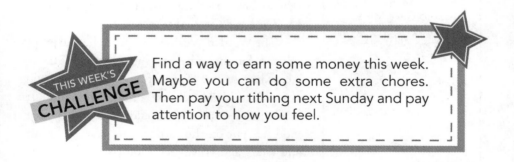

THIS WEEK'S CHALLENGE

Find a way to earn some money this week. Maybe you can do some extra chores. Then pay your tithing next Sunday and pay attention to how you feel.

WEEK 4

Prophets teach me to live the Word of Wisdom.

Lesson

In the early days of the Church, many of the brethren used tobacco during their meetings. One day Joseph Smith prayed about this and asked God if this was acceptable. Joseph received a revelation that we now call the Word of Wisdom, found in Doctrine and Covenants section 89.

The Word of Wisdom teaches us how to properly care for our bodies and show respect for them. According to the Word of Wisdom, we should not smoke, drink, or use drugs. We shouldn't drink coffee or tea. We should eat the foods that God has put on the earth for us, such as grains and fruits and vegetables. God has said that He put animals on the earth so we could have meat, but we should eat meat sparingly. If we follow the Word of Wisdom, we will receive many blessings. Our bodies will be healthy, and our minds will be filled with wisdom.

RESOURCES

(Select one from each category.)

Children's Songbook
The Lord Gave Me a Temple (153)
The Word of Wisdom (154)

Hymn
Keep the Commandments (303)
In Our Lovely Deseret (307)

Scriptures
Proverbs 20:1
1 Corinthians 3:17

Gospel Art Book
Brother Joseph (87)

Read and discuss Doctrine and Covenants 89:18–21.
How will we be blessed if we obey the Word of Wisdom?
How does the Word of Wisdom bless us both physically and spiritually?

Activity

Younger Children: Download and print the pictures on pages 58 and 59 from primaryhelper.com/downloads. Cut out the pictures of the food. Decide which foods are good for us and comply with the Word of Wisdom. Glue those pictures on the plate. Throw away the bad foods, such as alcohol, and explain that we should never have that. Explain that some foods, such as candy or fast food, are okay to eat sometimes. Choose one of those foods to glue on the plate, but throw the rest of them away.

Older Children: Make a nutritious snack or dessert that complies with the Word of Wisdom.

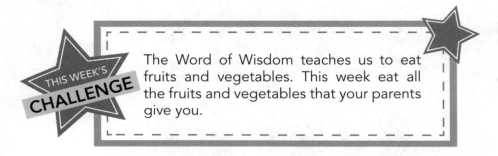

THIS WEEK'S CHALLENGE

The Word of Wisdom teaches us to eat fruits and vegetables. This week eat all the fruits and vegetables that your parents give you.

JUNE

I Will Follow Heavenly Father's Plan by Being Baptized and Confirmed

"Come unto me, and be baptized in my name, that ye may receive a remission of your sins, and be filled with the Holy Ghost" (3 Nephi 30:2).

WEEK 1

I will be baptized and confirmed and keep my baptismal covenants.

Lesson

When Jesus Christ was on the earth, He went to John the Baptist and asked to be baptized. At first John did not understand why Jesus wanted to be baptized, because Jesus did not have any sins. Jesus explained that He needed to be baptized "to fulfill all righteousness" (Matthew 3:15). Baptism is a commandment, and Jesus wanted to keep all the commandments.

Like Jesus, we all need to be baptized. When we are baptized, we show our commitment to follow Jesus Christ. We make covenants (sacred promises) to keep the commandments and be like Jesus. In the scriptures we learn that baptism is like a gate that opens up to heaven.

After we're baptized, we are confirmed and become members of The Church of Jesus Christ of Latter-day Saints. We also receive the gift of the

Holy Ghost. The Holy Ghost cleanses us from sin and purifies us. If we keep our baptismal covenants, we will be worthy to have the Holy Ghost as our constant companion to guide us and comfort us.

Read and discuss Mosiah 18:8–10.
What do we promise Heavenly Father when we are baptized?
What does Heavenly Father promise to do for us?

Activity

Younger Children: Draw or paint a picture of one of the ways you can keep your baptismal covenants.
Older Children: Do the crossword puzzle on page 64. You can download and print the activity at primaryhelper.com/downloads.

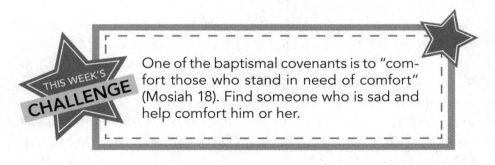

THIS WEEK'S CHALLENGE

One of the baptismal covenants is to "comfort those who stand in need of comfort" (Mosiah 18). Find someone who is sad and help comfort him or her.

CROSSWORD PUZZLE

Complete the crossword puzzle on the next page by filling in the missing words from the verses below. For example, 1A is the missing word that goes in 1 across, 2D is 2 down, and so forth. *Solution on page 137.*

Mosiah 18:8–10

8 And it came to pass that he said unto them: Behold, here are the waters of **(1D)** (for thus were they called) and now, as ye are desirous to come into the **(5A)** of God, and to be called his **(11D)**, and are willing to bear one another's **(16A)**, that they may be light;

9 Yea, and are willing to **(1A)** with those that mourn; yea, and comfort those that stand in need of **(12D)**, and to stand as **(17A)** of God at all **(13A)** and in all **(2D)**, and in all **(14A)** that ye

may be in, even until **(6D)**, that ye may be **(3D)** of God, and be numbered with those of the first resurrection, that ye may have eternal **(10A)**—

10 Now I say unto you, if this be the desire of your **(4A)**, what have you against being **(9A)** in the name of the Lord, as a witness before him that ye have entered into a **(7D)** with him, that ye will **(15D)** him and keep his **(12A)**, that he may pour out his **(8D)** more abundantly upon you?

WEEK 2

If I live worthily, the Holy Ghost will help me choose the right.

RESOURCES

(Select one from each category.)

Children's Songbook
The Holy Ghost (105)
The Still Small Voice (106)

Hymn
Let the Holy Spirit Guide (143)
The Light Divine (305)

Scriptures
D&C 8:2
D&C 121:45–46

Gospel Art Book
The Gift of the Holy Ghost (105)

Lesson

At times it can be hard to choose the right. Sometimes we don't know which choice is right. Other times we may know what choice we should make but want to do something else. We are blessed to have the Holy Ghost as our guide. The Holy Ghost can speak to us in a still, small voice and tell us what we should do.

One day you may be with your friends, and they may tell you to steal, make fun of another kid, or do something else you know is wrong. If you listen to the promptings from the Holy Ghost, you will feel a gentle nudge to do what Jesus would do.

We must be worthy to receive help from the Holy Ghost. Just as no unclean thing can dwell with God (see 1 Nephi 10:21), the Holy Ghost cannot dwell with us when we sin. The more we choose the right, the more the Holy Ghost will be with us to help us choose the right. We will always be safe and make the right decisions if we listen to the Holy Ghost.

Read and discuss 2 Nephi 32:5.
How do we receive the Holy Ghost?
How will the Holy Ghost show us what we must do?

Activity

Younger Children: Color the picture "My faith in Jesus Christ grows when I listen to the Holy Ghost" from the August 2007 *Friend* magazine. You can download it at lds.org/friend/2007/08/coloring-page?lang=eng.

Older Children: Do the crossword puzzle from the August 2007 *Friend* magazine. You can download it at lds.org/friend/2007/08/the-holy-ghost?lang=eng.

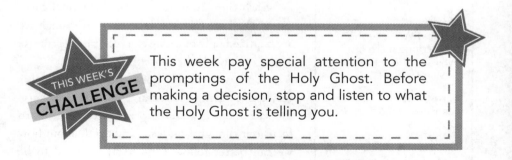

THIS WEEK'S CHALLENGE

This week pay special attention to the promptings of the Holy Ghost. Before making a decision, stop and listen to what the Holy Ghost is telling you.

RESOURCES

(Select one from
each category.)

Children's Songbook
The Sacrament (72)
Before I Take the
Sacrament (73a)

Hymn
As Now We Take the
Sacrament (169)
While of These Emblems
We Partake (173)

Scriptures
Matthew 26:26
D&C 59:9

Gospel Art Book
Blessing the Sacrament
(107)
Passing the Sacrament
(108)

WEEK 3

When I take the sacrament, I renew my baptismal covenants.

Lesson

When we are baptized, we promise to follow Jesus Christ. As much as we want to follow Him, we still sin afterward. Fortunately, we can always repent of our sins. We should repent often, even daily if necessary.

Each Sunday, we renew our baptismal covenants when we take the sacrament. Although we are baptized only once, we can recommit (promise again) each week to choose the right.

You have probably noticed that the chapel is very quiet during the sacrament. That is because the sacrament is a sacred ordinance. We need to focus our thoughts on Jesus and think about how we can better follow Him. And we need to be quiet so that those around us can do the same.

During the sacrament, some people read from the hymn book or from their scriptures. Others like to just think about what Jesus Christ means to them. Whatever you choose to do, make sure that your thoughts are focused on Jesus and His sacrifice for us. Think about what you can do that week to be a better disciple of Jesus Christ.

Read and discuss Doctrine and Covenants 20:77, 79.
What covenants do we renew when we take the sacrament?
What does God promise us if we keep our covenants?

Activity

All Ages: Look for pictures of the Savior in Church magazines. Cut them out and create a small book to look at while the sacrament is being passed. You could glue the pictures to several sheets of paper and then staple the papers together, or you could put the pictures in a binder or small photo album. If you don't want to cut your magazines, you can go to lds.org and download and print pictures.

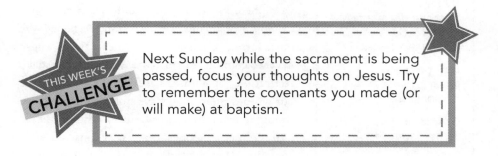

THIS WEEK'S CHALLENGE

Next Sunday while the sacrament is being passed, focus your thoughts on Jesus. Try to remember the covenants you made (or will make) at baptism.

WEEK 4

When I repent, I can be forgiven.

Lesson

RESOURCES

(Select one from each category.)

Children's Songbook
Repentance (98)
Help Me, Dear Father (99)

Hymn
Savior, Redeemer of My Soul (112)
Come unto Jesus (117)

Scriptures
Isaiah 1:18
3 Nephi 9:22

Gospel Art Book
Jesus Praying in Gethsemane (56)
Young Boy Praying (111)

No one is perfect. We all make mistakes and sin. Heavenly Father knew this would happen, so He provided a way for us to repent. The Atonement of Jesus Christ washes away our sins and makes us clean again, as if the sin never happened.

How do we repent? First, we must admit we have done something wrong and feel sorry that we sinned. Next, we must confess our sins both to God and anyone we have sinned against. We must forsake our sins, which means we promise never to commit the sin again. We must also make restitution. That means we should try to make our wrongs right. If we have stolen something, we should return it to the person from whom we stole it. If we hurt someone's feelings, we must sincerely apologize. If we have done all these things with a sincere heart, God will forgive us and remember our sins no more. It is important to repent daily and always keep the commandments the best we can. And we must be willing to forgive others in order for God to forgive us.

Read and discuss Mosiah 4:4–12.
What are the steps to repentance?
What happens to our sins when we repent?

Activity

All Ages: Watch a video about repentance at biblevideos.lds.org. Suggestions include "Go and Sin No More," "The Prodigal Son," and "The Savior Suffers in Gethsemane."

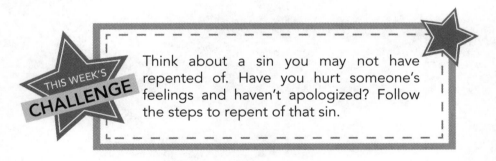

THIS WEEK'S CHALLENGE

Think about a sin you may not have repented of. Have you hurt someone's feelings and haven't apologized? Follow the steps to repent of that sin.

JULY

Families Are Part of
Heavenly Father's Plan

"The family is ordained of God"
("The Family: A Proclamation to the
World," paragraph 7).

WEEK 1

Heavenly Father planned for me to come to a family.

Lesson

Families are the most important part of Heavenly Father's plan for us. One of the first commandments Adam and Eve received was to have children. Heavenly Father wants His spirit children to come to earth and receive a body. When a married man and woman have children, they help Heavenly Father fulfill His plan.

Another purpose of families is to help each other make it back to Heavenly Father. Parents should teach their children the gospel and help them keep the commandments. But often children can teach their parents as well and be good examples to them.

Having a loving family brings one of the greatest joys in this life and in the life to come. When we love and serve our family members, we begin to understand the great love that Heavenly Father has for us.

RESOURCES

(Select one from each category.)

Children's Songbook
Love Is Spoken Here (190)
The Family (194)

Hymn
Love at Home (294)
Families Can Be Together Forever (300)

Scriptures
Ephesians 6:4
The Family: A Proclamation to the World

Gospel Art Book
Adam and Eve Teaching Their Children (5)
Family Prayer (112)

Read and discuss Doctrine and Covenants 88:119–26.
What can we do to have a successful family?
How can we show our family members that we love them?

Activity

Younger Children: Color the picture on page 76. You can download and print the activity at primaryhelper.com/downloads.

Older Children: Do the word search on page 77. You can download and print the activity at primaryhelper.com/downloads.

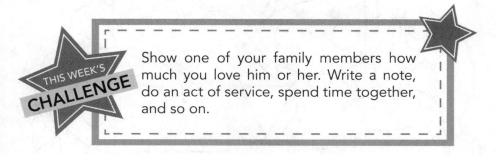

THIS WEEK'S CHALLENGE

Show one of your family members how much you love him or her. Write a note, do an act of service, spend time together, and so on.

Families Can Be Together Forever

WORD SEARCH
The Family: A Proclamation to the World

Below is an excerpt from "The Family: A Proclamation to the World." Find the words in bold in the word search. **Solution on page 137.**

Happiness in family life is most likely to be achieved when founded upon the teachings of the Lord Jesus Christ. Successful **marriages** and **families** are established and maintained on principles of **faith**, **prayer**, **repentance**, **forgiveness**, **respect**, **love**, **compassion**, **work**, and wholesome **recreational** activities.

```
F  I  W  H  A  P  P  I  N  E  S  S  R
A  C  D  D  Z  B  I  V  Y  R  X  G  E
M  I  O  W  A  A  A  H  C  E  T  Q  C
I  W  K  X  G  I  F  E  O  P  G  C  R
L  F  O  R  G  I  V  E  N  E  S  S  E
I  V  T  M  C  S  F  F  F  N  O  L  A
E  B  P  R  A  Y  E  R  O  T  N  G  T
S  G  A  E  S  X  K  H  I  A  Z  F  I
Z  P  V  W  O  R  K  P  Z  N  K  A  O
S  O  Y  W  V  Y  Y  Y  Q  C  O  I  N
L  R  R  E  S  P  E  C  T  E  U  T  A
R  C  O  M  P  A  S  S  I  O  N  H  L
Y  Y  X  M  A  R  R  I  A  G  E  S  U
```

WEEK 2

Family prayer, family scripture study, and FHE strengthen my family.

RESOURCES

(Select one from each category.)

Children's Songbook
Search, Ponder, and
   Pray (109)
Family Prayer (189)

Hymn
Did You Think to Pray?
   (140)
The Holy Word (279)

Scriptures
Luke 18:1
3 Nephi 18:15

Gospel Art Book
Family Prayer (112)

Lesson

We can do many things to strengthen our family. We can play together, go on vacation together, take walks together, and so forth. Spending time together as a family is very important. When we spend time together, we increase our love for each other.

Although the activities we mentioned are great ways to spend time together, Heavenly Father has asked us to do a few other things that are even more important. These things will help us grow together spiritually. The prophets have taught that we should have family prayer, family scripture study, and family home evening. It is very important to talk to Heavenly Father as a family and to learn about the gospel as a family. When we feel the Spirit together, we strengthen our eternal bonds. We learn how to help each other through trials and teach each other about Jesus Christ. Praying as a family and reading the scriptures together bring us together in a way that nothing else can.

Read and discuss 2 Nephi 32:3.
What does it mean to "feast upon the words of Christ"?
How will studying the scriptures strengthen our family?

Activity

All Ages: As a family, set a goal to hold family prayer, scripture study, and family home evening regularly. Then make a chart to keep track of your progress. Give yourself rewards when you reach your goal. For example, if your goal is to hold family home evening every week for a month, celebrate together at the end of the month if you've reached your goal. You could have ice cream, go on a family outing, play a game together, or do anything else that your family enjoys.

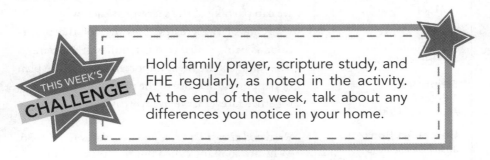

THIS WEEK'S CHALLENGE

Hold family prayer, scripture study, and FHE regularly, as noted in the activity. At the end of the week, talk about any differences you notice in your home.

WEEK 3

The priesthood can bless and strengthen my family.

Lesson

We are very lucky to have the priesthood on the earth today. Because of the priesthood, our family can be blessed and strengthened in many ways. It's wonderful to receive priesthood blessings when we are sick or need comfort and guidance. More important, because of the priesthood we can receive ordinances such as baptism, and we can partake of the sacrament each week.

One of the greatest blessings of the priesthood is being sealed to our families in the temple. The family is the most important part of the plan of happiness. Because of the priesthood, we can be together forever if we live worthily.

Read and discuss Doctrine and Covenants 121:34–36.
Why are so many called but few are chosen?
What does the following phrase mean: "the rights of the priesthood are inseparably connected with the powers of heaven"?

RESOURCES

(Select one from each category.)

Children's Songbook
The Priesthood Is Restored (89)
A Young Man Prepared (166)

Hymn
Truth Eternal (4)
Ye Elders of Israel (319)

Scriptures
1 Peter 2:9
Articles of Faith 1:5

Gospel Art Book
Jesus Blesses the Nephite Children (84)
Ordination to the Priesthood (106)

Activity

All Ages: Read and discuss the article "Blessed by the Priesthood" from the July 2006 *Friend* magazine, available at lds.org/liahona/2006/07/friend-to-friend-blessed-by-the-priesthood?lang=eng.

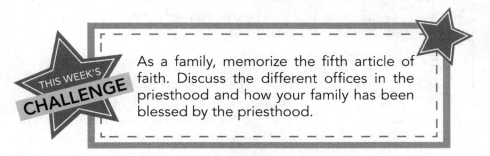

THIS WEEK'S CHALLENGE

As a family, memorize the fifth article of faith. Discuss the different offices in the priesthood and how your family has been blessed by the priesthood.

WEEK 4

Heavenly Father wants me to marry in the temple and have an eternal family.

RESOURCES

(Select one from each category.)

Children's Songbook
I Love to See the Temple (95)
Families Can Be Together Forever (188)

Hymn
High on the Mountain Top (5)
Families Can Be Together Forever (300)

Scriptures
D&C 132:19
The Family: A Proclamation to the World

Gospel Art Book
Salt Lake Temple (119)
Young Couple Going to the Temple (120)

Lesson

One of the most important commandments we can follow is to be married in the temple and have an eternal family. Marriage is an essential part of God's plan. In the Doctrine and Covenants, we learn that in order to obtain the highest degree of celestial glory we have to be married (see 131:1–3).

Many people in the world today don't think marriage is important. But we know from modern-day revelation that marriage is sacred. Heavenly Father wants us to be married so we can have a family and become more like Him.

In order to have an eternal marriage (a marriage that lasts forever), we have to be sealed in the temple. It is a sacred ordinance that must be performed by one who has the proper authority.

When we are sealed in the temple, our families can be together forever, even after we die. It is one of the greatest gifts Heavenly Father offers us.

Read and discuss Doctrine and Covenants 49:15.
Why does God want us to get married?
What are some of the blessings of marriage?

Activity

All Ages: Play a matching game with the pictures of the temples on pages 84 and 85. Print the cards, cut them out, turn them face down on a table, and see who can get the most matches. You can download and print the activity at pimaryhelper. com/downloads.

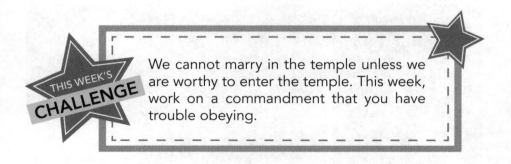

THIS WEEK'S CHALLENGE

We cannot marry in the temple unless we are worthy to enter the temple. This week, work on a commandment that you have trouble obeying.

AUGUST

Heavenly Father Hears and Answers My Prayers

"Be thou humble, and the Lord thy God
shall lead thee by the hand, and give
thee answer to thy prayers"
(D&C 112:10).

WEEK 1

The scriptures teach me how to pray.

RESOURCES

(Select one from each category.)

Children's Songbook
We Bow Our Heads (25a)
I Love to Pray (25b)

Hymn
Sweet Hour of Prayer (142)
Secret Prayer (144)

Scriptures
Matthew 6:9–13
Luke 21:36

Gospel Art Book
Enos Praying (72)

Lesson

In the Book of Mormon we read about a man named Enos and his experience with prayer. One day Enos was hunting in the forest and started thinking about the gospel truths that his father, Jacob, had taught him. Enos felt a great desire in his heart to repent of his sins. He knelt down in the forest and began to pray. Let's read about his experience.

Read and discuss Enos 1:1–17.
What are some of the things Enos prayed for?
How did Enos feel when he prayed?

Activity

Younger Children: Color the picture "We Do Not Doubt" from the March 2010 *Friend* magazine, available at lds.org/bc/content/shared/content/images/gospel-library/magazine/fr10mar35_dots.jpg.

Older Children: Complete the activity "Picture Puzzle" from the October 2016 *Friend* magazine. You can download and print the activity at media.ldscdn.org/pdf/magazines/friend-october-2016/2016-10-09-funstuff-picture-puzzle-eng.pdf.

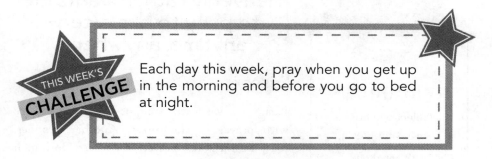

THIS WEEK'S CHALLENGE

Each day this week, pray when you get up in the morning and before you go to bed at night.

WEEK 2

Heavenly Father wants me to pray to Him often— anytime, anywhere.

Lesson

Last week we learned about Enos's experience with prayer in the forest. Another prophet, Joseph Smith, also prayed in a forest. Both men had wonderful experiences. From them we can learn that we don't have to be at home or at church in order to pray. Heavenly Father wants us to pray to Him often—anytime, anywhere.

It's important to find a quiet place to pray so that we can listen to the whisperings of the Spirit. But sometimes that isn't possible. Sometimes we need help immediately and can't go anywhere to be alone. During those times we can say a quiet prayer in our hearts. Maybe we're taking a test at school and forgot what we studied. We can say a prayer in our heart for help. Or maybe during a hard day we're on the playground and someone smiles at us and makes us feel better. We can say a prayer in our heart to thank Heavenly Father for that person. It doesn't matter where we are. Heavenly Father will still hear and answer our prayers.

Read and discuss 1 Thessalonians 5:17.
What does it mean to "pray without ceasing"?
Where and when can we pray?

Activity

Younger Children: The little girl on page 92 is saying a prayer. Draw a picture inside of the thought bubble of something you think she is praying for. You can download and print the activity at primaryhelper.com/downloads.

Older Children: Do the word puzzle on page 93. You can download and print the activity at primaryhelper.com/downloads.

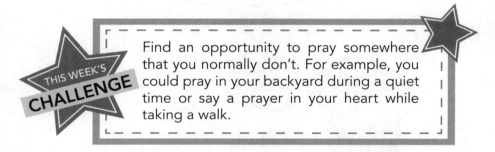

THIS WEEK'S CHALLENGE

Find an opportunity to pray somewhere that you normally don't. For example, you could pray in your backyard during a quiet time or say a prayer in your heart while taking a walk.

PRAYER SCRAMBLE

Unscramble the words to find out what this girl is praying for. *Solution on page 137.*

1. YAMFIL
2. MEOH
3. EDNFIRS
4. NAMAISL
5. EALHTH
6. SIWMOD

1. _____

2. _____

3. _____

4. _____

5. _____

6. _____

WEEKS 3&4

Answers to prayers come in many different ways.

RESOURCES

(Select one from each category.)

Children's Songbook
I Feel My Savior's Love (74)
Search, Ponder, and Pray (109)

Hymn
Be Thou Humble (130)
Softly Now the Light of Day (160)

Scriptures
Matthew 7:7
Matthew 21:22

Gospel Art Book
Young Boy Praying (111)
Family Prayer (112)

Lesson

Heavenly Father always hears and answers our prayers. It can be difficult to know if we have received an answer, so it's important to know the different ways Heavenly Father can answer our prayers.

Sometimes when we pray, we need Heavenly Father to tell us "yes" or "no." In the Doctrine and Covenants we learn that we must first think about what decision we should make. If the answer is yes, we will feel a burning in our bosom. If the answer is no, we will receive a stupor of thought (see D&C 9:8–9).

We can receive answers to our prayers in many other ways as well. Sometimes we may have a question and then find the answer while we're reading the scriptures. Sometimes we may pray for help, and one of our friends will call or visit us and know exactly what to do. Sometimes we will feel strongly that we need to do certain things.

There are many more ways in which Heavenly Father can answer our prayers. It can be different for each person, so it is important to pray often. By praying often and listening for answers, we can learn how Heavenly Father speaks to us.

Read and discuss Doctrine and Covenants 8:2.
According to this verse, how does Heavenly Father answer prayers?
What are some other ways that He answers our prayers?

Activity

Younger Children: Do the puzzle on page 96. You can download and print the activity at primaryhelper.com/downloads.
Older Children: Have a scripture chase using scriptures that talk about prayer. Use the Topical Guide for help.

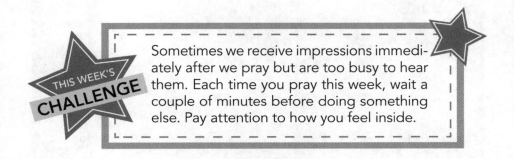

THIS WEEK'S CHALLENGE

Sometimes we receive impressions immediately after we pray but are too busy to hear them. Each time you pray this week, wait a couple of minutes before doing something else. Pay attention to how you feel inside.

SEPTEMBER

I Will Serve God with All My Heart, Might, Mind, and Strength

"Thou shalt love the Lord thy God with all thy heart, with all thy might, mind, and strength; and in the name of Jesus Christ thou shalt serve him" (D&C 59:5).

WEEK 1

Jesus Christ taught us how to serve others.

Lesson

RESOURCES

(Select one from each category.)

Children's Songbook
I'm Trying to Be like Jesus (78)
I'll Walk with You (140)

Hymn
Have I Done Any Good? (223)
Scatter Sunshine (230)

Scriptures
Ephesians 2:10
D&C 64:33

Gospel Art Book
The Ten Lepers (46)
Jesus Washing the Apostles' Feet (55)

Jesus spent His life serving others. He loved everyone, even the outcasts. One day He went to a small town and met ten lepers. These men had sores all over their bodies. No one would help the lepers because everyone was afraid of getting the terrible disease. But Jesus did not turn them away. When the lepers asked Him to heal them, He lovingly did so. Jesus told the lepers to go to the priests. On the way there, they were healed. But only one leper returned to thank Jesus.

We can learn two important lessons from this story. First, Jesus did not turn the lepers away. Even though others were afraid of them, Jesus was kind to them and healed them. Second, Jesus did not expect anything in return. Although he was disappointed that only one leper thanked Him, He probably knew before He healed the lepers that not all of them would return. But He healed them anyway because He loved them and wanted them to be well. Jesus was the perfect example of how to love and serve others.

Read and discuss Matthew 5:16.
What is the light that Jesus is speaking of?
How can we let our lights shine?
What can we do to follow Jesus's example and serve others?

Activity

All Ages: As a family, brainstorm at least ten different ideas for service projects you can do together. (You will do one of the service projects next week.)

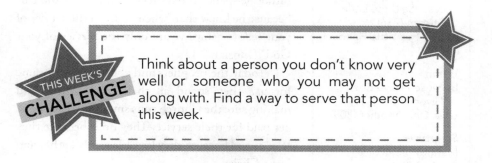

THIS WEEK'S CHALLENGE

Think about a person you don't know very well or someone who you may not get along with. Find a way to serve that person this week.

WEEK 2

Prophets and apostles show us how to serve.

Lesson

In the Book of Mormon, King Benjamin, who was also a prophet, taught a great lesson about service. Even though he was the king, he worked alongside the people. He didn't tax or enslave them, but rather he spent his days serving them. He did this because he knew that "when ye are in the service of your fellow beings ye are only the service of your God" (Mosiah 2:17).

Today the prophets and apostles do the same for us. They spend all their time serving and making sure the Church runs smoothly. They don't get paid for their service. They do it because they love us and because they love Heavenly Father and Jesus Christ.

Read and discuss Mosiah 2:11–14.
What did King Benjamin do for his people?
What can we learn from his example?

RESOURCES

(Select one from each category.)

Children's Songbook
"Give," Said the Little Stream (236)
I Have Two Little Hands (272)

Hymn
Because I Have Been Given Much (219)
Love One Another (308)

Scriptures
Matthew 25:40
D&C 42:31

Gospel Art Book
King Benjamin Addresses His People (74)
Thomas S. Monson (137)

Activity

All Ages: Do one of the service projects that your family talked about last week.

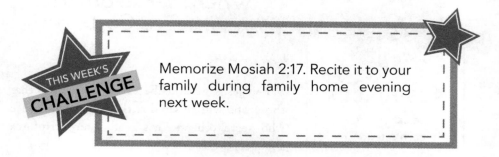

THIS WEEK'S CHALLENGE

Memorize Mosiah 2:17. Recite it to your family during family home evening next week.

WEEKS 3&4

When I serve others, I serve God.

RESOURCES

(Select one from each category.)

Children's Songbook
Where Love Is (138)
Go the Second Mile (167)

Hymn
Let Us All Press On (243)
As Sisters in Zion (309)

Scriptures
Mosiah 2:17
D&C 42:30–31

Gospel Art Book
The Good Samaritan (44)
Service (115)

Lesson

When Jesus was on the earth, He taught that those who will be saved at the last day are those who serve others. Let's read some scriptures about service.

Read and discuss Matthew 25:34–40.
What did Jesus mean when He said, "Inasmuch as ye have done it unto one of the least of these my brethren, ye have done it unto me?"
How can we serve our family members?
How are we serving God when we serve others?

Read and discuss the parable of the good Samaritan in Luke 10:25–37.
According to the parable, who are our neighbors?
How did the good Samaritan help his neighbor?
How do we love our neighbors as ourselves? How can we serve them?

Activity

All Ages: Pick one of your neighbors to "heart attack." Cut out a dozen or more hearts from colored paper and secretly tape the hearts to your neighbor's front door. If you'd like, you can write messages on the hearts and leave a plate of treats. See page 104 if you need a template for the hearts. You can download and print them at primaryhelper.com/downloads.

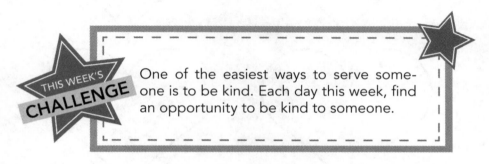

THIS WEEK'S CHALLENGE

One of the easiest ways to serve someone is to be kind. Each day this week, find an opportunity to be kind to someone.

OCTOBER

I Will Share the Gospel with All of God's Children

"Let your light so shine before men, that they may see your good works, and glorify your Father which is in heaven" (Matthew 5:16).

WEEKS 1&2

Living the gospel helps me to be a missionary now.

Lesson

The prophets have taught that every member should be a missionary. Did you know that you don't have to serve a mission to do that? Sometimes you don't even have to open your mouth. When you live the gospel and set a good example, you show others how to follow Jesus Christ.

What would you do if you were around a group of children who were teasing another child? The right thing to do would be to ask them to stop and to help the child being teased to feel loved. By doing so, you would show the other children how Jesus wants us to treat each other.

What would you do if your friend dared you to steal something? By saying no, you would show your friend that you know that stealing is wrong.

We don't always have to be at church or have a formal lesson to teach someone about Jesus. When we set a good example, we show others how to follow Him.

RESOURCES

(Select one from each category.)

Children's Songbook
I Want to Be a
  Missionary Now (168)
I Hope They Call Me on
  a Mission (169)

Hymn
We Are Sowing (216)
Each Life That Touches
  Ours for Good (293)

Scriptures
1 Timothy 4:12
Mosiah 18:9

Gospel Art Book
Missionaries: Elders (109)
Missionaries: Sisters (110)

Read and discuss Doctrine and Covenants 18:10–15.
How much is a soul worth to God?
Why will we experience great joy if we bring even one soul unto repentance?

Activity

Younger Children: Draw a picture and send it to a missionary.
Older Children: Write a letter to a missionary.

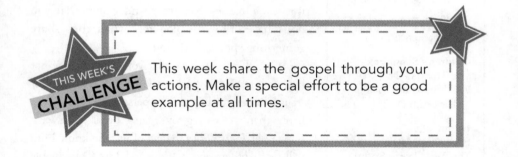

THIS WEEK'S CHALLENGE

This week share the gospel through your actions. Make a special effort to be a good example at all times.

WEEK 3

I can share the gospel with my family and friends.

Lesson

What do you like about going to your friends' houses? Do they have toys and games that you don't have? How do you feel when they share something special with you?

One thing you have that your friends may not have is a testimony of Jesus Christ. A testimony of Jesus Christ is the best thing a person can have—even better than an exciting toy, a fancy dress, or a swimming pool. Jesus hopes that all of us who know Him will teach others about Him and His Church. He loves each of us very much and wants us to return to Him.

But He needs our help. He needs us to share our testimonies with our friends and invite them to church with us. He wants us to help them feel how much He loves them.

RESOURCES

(Select one from each category.)

Children's Songbook
The Things I Do (170)
We'll Bring the World His Truth (172)

Hymn
Hark, All Ye Nations! (264)
The Time Is Far Spent (266)

Scriptures
Mark 16:15
D&C 88:81

Gospel Art Book
Missionaries: Elders (109)
Missionaries: Sisters (110)

It can be scary to talk to our friends about Jesus. But Jesus has promised that He will help us have the courage to do it and know what to say.

Read and discuss Doctrine and Covenants 84:85.
Why shouldn't we worry about what we will say?
How can we prepare ourselves to share the gospel?

Activity

All Ages: Invite a returned missionary to come to your house and share some of his or her mission experiences. Ask them about the people they taught, the country in which they served, and the customs of the people there.

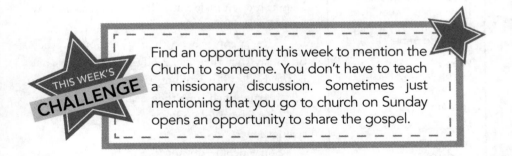

THIS WEEK'S CHALLENGE

Find an opportunity this week to mention the Church to someone. You don't have to teach a missionary discussion. Sometimes just mentioning that you go to church on Sunday opens an opportunity to share the gospel.

WEEK 4

My testimony is strengthened when I share the gospel.

Lesson

We have to use our muscles if we want them to get stronger. The same is true with our testimony. We have to share it in order to strengthen it. If we keep it hidden inside, it will get weaker and may even die.

After people bear their testimonies, they often say that they feel really good inside. That is the Holy Ghost telling them that what they said is true. Each time they bear their testimony and feel the Holy Ghost, their testimony is strengthened.

Some people do not like to bear their testimony because they are afraid and unsure of what to say. Heavenly Father has promised that He will help us. He will give us the right words to say exactly when we need them.

Read and discuss 2 Timothy 1:8.
What does it mean to be "ashamed of the testimony of our Lord"?
How will Heavenly Father help you bear your testimony?

Activity

All Ages: Invite the missionaries over for dinner. Ask them about their teaching experiences and how you can help share the gospel.

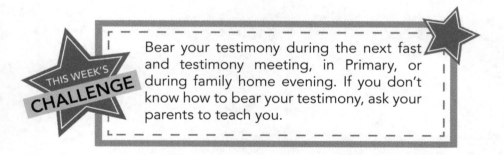

THIS WEEK'S CHALLENGE

Bear your testimony during the next fast and testimony meeting, in Primary, or during family home evening. If you don't know how to bear your testimony, ask your parents to teach you.

NOVEMBER

We Are to Thank God in All Things

"He commanded them that . . . every day they should give thanks to the Lord their God" (Mosiah 18:23).

WEEK 1

I am thankful for my body, and I know that it is a temple.

RESOURCES

(Select one from each category.)

Children's Songbook
For Health and Strength (21a)
The Lord Gave Me a Temple (153)

Hymn
For All the Saints (82)
We Love Thy House, O God (247)

Scriptures
Romans 12:1
D&C 93:35

Lesson

Our bodies are a wonderful gift from Heavenly Father. In the New Testament, the Apostle Paul compared our bodies to a temple (see 1 Corinthians 3:16). The temple is the house of God, and our bodies are the house of our spirits and a place where the Holy Ghost can dwell.

Our bodies are sacred, and we need to take good care of them. Just as we would never defile the temple, we should never defile our bodies. How would you feel if someone drew all over your favorite toy with a permanent marker or broke it in half? You'd probably be pretty sad. That's how Heavenly Father feels when we don't take care of our bodies.

The prophet has taught that we should dress modestly and live the Word of Wisdom. When we do so, we show respect for our bodies and show Heavenly Father that we are thankful for them.

Read and discuss 1 Corinthians 3:16.
How are our bodies like temples?
How can we show that we are thankful for our bodies?

Activity

Younger Children: The pictures on page 116 show ways we can take good care of our bodies. In the center of the pictures, draw your own picture of another way you can take care of your body. You can download and print the activity at primaryhelper.com/downloads.

Older Children: See page 117. You can download and print the activity at primaryhelper.com/downloads.

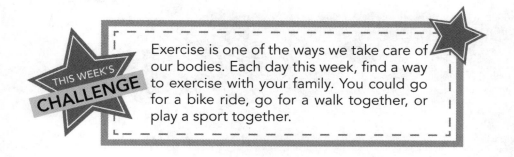

THIS WEEK'S CHALLENGE

Exercise is one of the ways we take care of our bodies. Each day this week, find a way to exercise with your family. You could go for a bike ride, go for a walk together, or play a sport together.

PICTURE MATCH

These children are taking care of their bodies by exercising. Find the child that is the same in each picture. *Solution on page 137.*

WEEK 2

I am thankful for temporal blessings.

Lesson

Heavenly Father has blessed us with many things. In fact, everything we have comes from Him. We may not realize it, but even temporal blessings come from Him. Temporal blessings are things we can see and touch, such as our home, car, food, and so on. Even less important objects such as toys can be a temporal blessing.

What are some of the temporal blessings you are thankful for? *(Spend a few minutes discussing temporal blessings. Have each member of the family list three things they are thankful for.)*

Read and discuss Doctrine and Covenants 46:7.
How does God give liberally?
How do we do things with prayer and thanksgiving?

RESOURCES

(Select one from each category.)

Children's Songbook
A Song of Thanks (20a)
I Am Glad for Many Things (151)

Hymn
There Is Sunshine in My Soul Today (227)
Count Your Blessings (241)

Scriptures
Psalm 95:2
D&C 136:28

Activity

All Ages: Show your gratitude for someone by writing a thank you note.

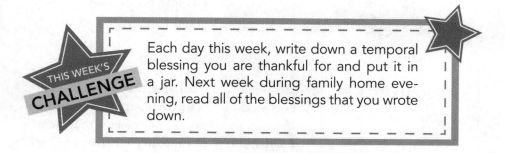

THIS WEEK'S CHALLENGE

Each day this week, write down a temporal blessing you are thankful for and put it in a jar. Next week during family home evening, read all of the blessings that you wrote down.

WEEK 3

I am thankful for spiritual blessings.

Lesson

Last week we talked about temporal blessings. This week, let's talk about spiritual blessings. Spiritual blessings are not objects that we can touch and feel, but rather gifts from the Holy Ghost and the priesthood. A testimony is an example of a spiritual blessing. Through the power of the Holy Ghost, we are blessed with a knowledge of Jesus Christ. Other spiritual blessings include the Atonement, sacred ordinances, and the sealing power that binds families together forever.

What are some of the spiritual blessings you are thankful for? (*Spend a few minutes discussing spiritual blessings. Implementing this week's activity, have each member of the family list three spiritual blessings they are thankful for.*)

RESOURCES

(Select one from each category.)

Children's Songbook
I Thank Thee, Dear Father (7)
I'm Thankful to Be Me (11)

Hymn
All Creatures of Our God and King (62)
Now Thank We All Our God (95)

Scriptures
Psalm 100:4
Philippians 4:6

Read and discuss Psalm 147:7.
What does it mean to "sing unto the Lord with thanksgiving"?
What are some ways you can show Heavenly Father you are thankful?

Activity

All Ages: Play Thankful Ball. A parent starts by tossing a ball to one of the children (Player 1), who has to name a spiritual blessing. Player 1 then tosses the ball to another child (Player 2), who names a different spiritual blessing. If Player 2 cannot come up with an answer, he returns the ball to Player 1, who tosses the ball to someone else. The game ends after everyone has named three spiritual blessings.

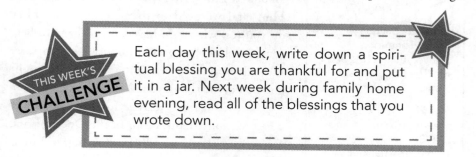

THIS WEEK'S CHALLENGE

Each day this week, write down a spiritual blessing you are thankful for and put it in a jar. Next week during family home evening, read all of the blessings that you wrote down.

WEEK 4

We should thank Heavenly Father for all our blessings.

Lesson

RESOURCES

(Select one from each category.)

Children's Songbook
Thank Thee for Everything (10)
For Thy Bounteous Blessings (21b)

Hymn
Prayer of Thanksgiving (93)
Come, Ye Thankful People (94)

Scriptures
Psalm 50:14
1 Timothy 4:4

Gospel Art Book
Young Boy Praying (111)
Family Prayer (112)

This month we have discussed gratitude, or being thankful. We should thank Heavenly Father for all our blessings. Everything we have comes from Him, and we need to thank Him often. How do you feel when you have worked hard to help someone and that person doesn't seem to care? How do you feel when you give someone a gift and he doesn't thank you? You feel hurt and disappointed. Heavenly Father feels the same way when we don't thank Him. In the Doctrine and Covenants, the Lord tells us that ingratitude is one of the greatest sins: "And in nothing doth man offend God, or against none is his wrath kindled, save those who confess not his hand in all things, and obey not his commandments" (59:21).

In the Book of Mormon, Amulek teaches that we should thank God daily for our blessings. Let's read what he said in Alma 34:38.

Read and discuss Alma 34:38.
How do we live in thanksgiving daily?
What are some of the mercies God has bestowed upon you?

Activity

All Ages: Print out the picture on page 124. In the box, make a list of what you are thankful for. (You may also draw pictures of things you are thankful for.) Put the turkey on the fridge or somewhere you will see it often. Each time you look at it, think about all of the blessings God has given you. You can download and print the activity at primaryhelper.com/downloads.

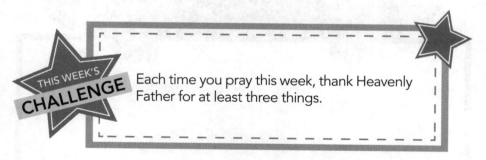

THIS WEEK'S CHALLENGE

Each time you pray this week, thank Heavenly Father for at least three things.

DECEMBER

I Know That Jesus Christ Will Come Again

"I know that my redeemer liveth, and
that he shall stand at the latter day
upon the earth" (Job 19:25).

WEEK 1

The prophets foretold that Jesus Christ would come to earth.

Lesson

Since the beginning of time, the prophets have taught that someday Jesus Christ would come to the earth to be our Savior. Isaiah, an Old Testament prophet, had many beautiful prophecies about the Savior. One of them is found in Isaiah 9: "For unto us a child is born, unto us a son is given: and the government shall be upon his shoulder: and his name shall be called Wonderful, Counsellor, The mighty God, The everlasting Father, The Prince of Peace" (v. 6). The prophets taught that Jesus would be born a baby, just like the rest of us. But He would be different from the rest of us because He would have a special mission to fulfill. He would be the Savior of the World. He would make it possible for us to overcome sin and death and return to our Father in Heaven. Let's read about the Savior's birth in Luke 2.

Read and discuss the birth of Jesus in Luke 2:1–19.
Why did the angel tell the shepherds not to fear?
Why was Jesus born in a manger?

Activity

Younger Children: See page 128. You can download and print the activity at primaryhelper.com/downloads.

Older Children: See page 129. You can download and print the activity at primaryhelper.com/downloads.

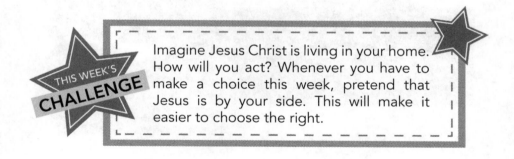

THIS WEEK'S CHALLENGE

Imagine Jesus Christ is living in your home. How will you act? Whenever you have to make a choice this week, pretend that Jesus is by your side. This will make it easier to choose the right.

3D Nativity Scene

1 print   2 cut out   3 assemble
- - - - - CUT LINES   - - - - - FOLD LINES

WORD SEARCH

Find the words in the word search. Remember, words may appear forward, backward, horizontally, vertically, or diagonally. *Solution on page 137.*

STAR
SHEPHERD
MARY
JOSEPH
JESUS
ANGEL
WISE MEN
STABLE
MANGER

G	P	Q	X	A	N	G	E	L	M	N
U	Y	K	A	F	J	C	W	S	M	C
Q	Q	L	E	L	Y	D	J	S	A	C
R	Z	Y	F	F	P	K	O	H	N	I
N	S	T	A	B	L	E	S	E	G	Q
G	K	M	S	Q	Y	U	E	P	E	X
S	F	M	G	R	S	N	P	H	R	C
X	Y	O	A	E	P	R	H	E	Z	V
Z	V	M	J	Q	O	J	Z	R	S	K
W	I	S	E	M	E	N	P	D	F	Q
C	S	T	A	R	I	L	E	Y	D	O

WEEK 2

Jesus Christ will come to the earth again.

Lesson

After Jesus was resurrected, He taught His disciples that even though He would soon return to His father, He would come to earth again. But no one would know when that would be. Jesus said, "But of that day and hour knoweth no man, no, not the angels of heaven, but my Father only" (Matthew 24:36). Latter-day prophets have taught that the Second Coming will take place soon. But we still do not know when that day will come. We need to live righteously and be ready to meet Jesus. It will be a glorious day for those who are prepared.

When Jesus comes again, He will establish His kingdom here on earth. We must be prepared for that day because only the righteous will remain on the earth. Even though we don't know exactly when Jesus will return, we have many scriptures that tell us which signs to look for.

Read and discuss Matthew 24. (It's a long chapter, so read it beforehand and select verses to read with your family.)

What are some of the signs of the Second Coming?

How can we prepare for it?

Activity

All Ages: Print and cut out the ornaments on page 136. On each ornament write something you can do to prepare for the Second Coming. Tape the ornaments to your door, a mirror, or somewhere you will see them often to remind you to work on those things. You can download and print the activity at primaryhelper.com/downloads.

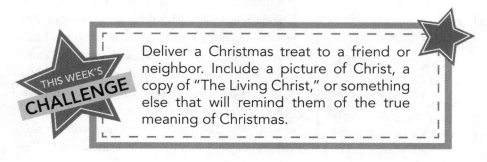

THIS WEEK'S CHALLENGE

Deliver a Christmas treat to a friend or neighbor. Include a picture of Christ, a copy of "The Living Christ," or something else that will remind them of the true meaning of Christmas.

WEEK 3

I will prepare to live with Heavenly Father and Jesus Christ again.

Lesson

Jesus Christ loves us very much. Through the Atonement, He made it possible for us to be resurrected and live with Him again someday. But we must do our part. We must have faith in Jesus Christ, repent of our sins, and keep the commandments. We must do all we can to follow His example and endure to the end. Living with Jesus Christ and Heavenly Father again is called eternal life. They want very much to give this gift to us. In Moses 1:39, the Lord said, "For behold, this is my work and my glory—to bring to pass the immortality and eternal life of man." That means Heavenly Father and Jesus Christ are working very hard to help us make it back to our heavenly home.

Do you remember when we learned about Enos? After he prayed all day and all night, he received forgiveness for his sins. When he grew older, he knew he would soon die. But he was not afraid because he knew he had lived a good life and would be with Jesus Christ again.

Read and discuss Enos 1:27.
Why wasn't Enos afraid to die?
What did he mean when he said he would rest in his Redeemer?
How can we have strong faith like Enos had?

Activity

All Ages: Have each family member write down something they can give Jesus for Christmas. Put the slips of paper in a box, and then wrap the box and put it under the Christmas tree. On Christmas Eve or Christmas morning, open the box and read aloud what each family member is giving to Jesus.

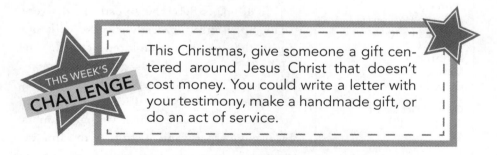

THIS WEEK'S CHALLENGE

This Christmas, give someone a gift centered around Jesus Christ that doesn't cost money. You could write a letter with your testimony, make a handmade gift, or do an act of service.

WEEK 4

I have a testimony that I am a child of God.

Lesson

This year we have learned that we are children of God. We have a loving Heavenly Father who wants to bless us and help us return to Him. At times it may be hard to believe that He really knows us because we cannot see Him. What do you think you should do if you want to gain a testimony that you are a child of God?

In Romans 8:16 the Apostle Paul wrote, "The Spirit itself beareth witness with our spirit, that we are the children of God." The Holy Ghost can help us gain a testimony. When the Holy Ghost speaks to our spirits, it is more powerful than if we were talking to someone face to face. When we have doubts, Heavenly Father wants us to pray to Him. He answers us by sending the Holy Ghost to testify of truth and help us understand the words of the prophets and the scriptures.

RESOURCES

(Select one from each category.)

Children's Songbook
I Am a Child of God (2)
I Know My Father Lives (5)

Hymn
Father in Heaven (133)
O My Father (292)

Scriptures
Matthew 5:48
Galatians 4:7

Gospel Art Book
Jesus Christ (1)

When the Holy Ghost speaks to us, we feel peace and the love of our Heavenly Father. It becomes easier to know that we are indeed children of God.

Read and discuss Doctrine and Covenants 84:83.
What do you think Heavenly Father knows about you and what you need?
How does it make you feel to know that you are a child of God and He knows you so well?

Activity

All Ages: Celebrate the end of the year with your family. Make your favorite recipe from the back of this book and play your favorite game together.

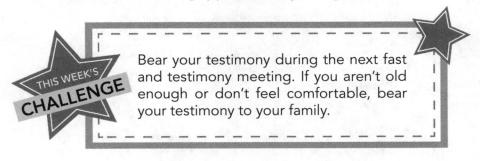

THIS WEEK'S CHALLENGE

Bear your testimony during the next fast and testimony meeting. If you aren't old enough or don't feel comfortable, bear your testimony to your family.

ANSWER KEY

PAGE 5

God is my Heavenly Father. He knows and loves me.

PAGE 17

PAGE 23

PAGE 26

Adam fell that men might be; and men are, that they might have joy.

PAGE 31

PAGE 49

Joseph Smith was a prophet of God. He translated the Book of Mormon and restored gospel truths.

PAGE 65

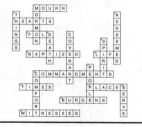

PAGE 77

PAGE 93

1. FAMILY
2. HOME
3. FRIENDS
4. ANIMALS
5. HEALTH
6. WISDOM

PAGE 117

PAGE 129

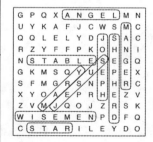

FUN FOOD
FOR FHE

Simple, Kid-Friendly Recipes

Resurrection Rolls

1 can refrigerated biscuits
  (liken them to the wrapping of Jesus's body and the tomb)
1/2 cup butter, melted
  (liken them to the oils used for anointing)
1/4 cup sugar mixed with 2 Tbsp. cinnamon
  (liken them to the spices for embalming)
1 marshmallow for each biscuit
  (liken them to Jesus's body)

1. Flatten each biscuit until it is large enough to wrap around a marshmallow.
2. Dip a marshmallow in butter and then roll it in the cinnamon-sugar mixture until it is completely covered.
3. Place the marshmallow in the center of a flattened biscuit. Pinch the dough around the marshmallow to seal it inside. Be sure not to leave any holes or else the marshmallow will leak out during baking.
4. Dip the dough ball into butter and then roll in cinnamon and sugar.
5. Repeat for the remaining biscuits and marshmallows.
6. Place each dough ball on a greased cookie sheet. Bake at 375 degrees for 10 minutes, or until the rolls are golden brown. Cool before eating.
7. When the rolls have cooled, break one in half to show your children that the marshmallow is gone. Liken this to the empty tomb when Jesus was resurrected.

Vanilla Ice Cream in a Jar

1 pint heavy cream

1 tsp. vanilla

1/4 cup sugar

1. Pour the pint of cream into a 1-quart jar.
2. Add vanilla and sugar.
3. Place the lid on the jar and seal well. Shake the jar for 5 minutes or until the cream solidifies.
4. Place a wet paper towel around the jar. Put the jar in the freezer for 2–3 hours.

Watermelon Frozen Yogurt

6 cups frozen watermelon cubes
1 cup vanilla yogurt

1. Place the frozen watermelon cubes into a food processor and process until the watermelon breaks down and becomes grainy. Slowly add the yogurt and process until the mixture is creamy.

NOTE: You most likely will not be able to make the entire recipe at once. It all depends on the size of your food processor. You may have to make half at a time or even one-fourth at a time.

Oreo Truffle Bites

1 pkg. Oreo cookies
1 (8-oz.) pkg. cream cheese, softened
24 oz. chocolate chips (white, dark, or milk)

1. Put the Oreos in a blender or food processor and pulse until no big pieces remain.
2. Pour the crushed Oreos into a large mixing bowl and mix thoroughly with the softened cream cheese.
3. Scoop dough by tablespoonfuls and roll into balls.
4. Melt the chocolate chips in the microwave at 50 percent power in 30-second intervals, stirring between intervals.
5. Put a dough ball on a fork and dip it in the chocolate until completely covered. Place it on a plate or a cookie sheet. Repeat until all of the dough balls have been dipped.
6. Put the truffles in the fridge for one hour or until they are thoroughly chilled.

Easy Caramel Apple Cake

2 cans apple pie filling
1/2 cup caramel syrup
1 box white cake mix
1/2 cup butter, melted

1. Preheat the oven to 350 degrees. Spray a 9x13-inch baking dish with cooking spray. Spread the pie filling over the bottom of the dish.
2. Drizzle the caramel sauce over the pie filling.
3. Top the pie filling with the dry cake mix.
4. Pour the melted butter over the top. If necessary, tilt the pan to cover the cake mix as evenly as possible.
5. Bake for 40–45 minutes. If desired, serve with whipped cream or vanilla ice cream.

Chocolate Mousse in a Jar

1 cup heavy cream
1/4 cup unsweetened cocoa powder
2 Tbsp. powdered sugar

1. Place all of the ingredients in a jar and seal the lid tightly.
2. Shake the jar for two minutes. If you want your mousse thicker, shake the jar a little longer.

Frozen Yogurt Bark

2 cups yogurt (any flavor)
1 Tbsp. each of the following: chocolate chips, chopped
    berries, shredded coconut, nuts, or dried fruit

1. Line a baking tray with foil. Spread the yogurt evenly on top.
2. Sprinkle with chocolate chips and other toppings.
3. Put in freezer until completely frozen (about 2–4 hours).
4. Using a sharp knife, break the bark into pieces.

Chocolate Cherry Cake

2 cans cherry pie filling
1 box chocolate cake mix
3/4 cup butter, melted

1. Preheat the oven to 350 degrees. Spray a 9x13-inch baking dish with cooking spray. Spread the pie filling over the bottom of the dish.
2. Top the pie filling with the cake mix.
3. Pour the melted butter over the top. If necessary, tilt the pan to cover the cake mix as evenly as possible.
4. Bake for 40–45 minutes. If desired, serve with whipped cream or vanilla ice cream.

Brownie Waffles

1 packaged brownie mix
1/4 cup water
2 eggs
1/2 cup oil

1. Mix the brownies according to the package directions. If the measurements for the water, eggs, and oil are different than what is listed above, use the measurements listed on the box.
2. Instead of baking, pour batter into a waffle iron. Cook for 3–4 minutes.
3. Eat your brownie waffle plain or top with ice cream, whipped cream, hot fudge, and so on.

Strawberry Poke Cake

1 box white cake mix
1 (3-oz.) pkg. strawberry Jell-O
1 cup boiling water
1 container whipped topping
Sliced strawberries

1. Bake the cake mix according to the package directions. Cool for 5–10 minutes.
2. Using a chopstick, straw, or the end of a wooden spoon, poke holes all over the cake.
3. Boil 1 cup of water and mix it with the strawberry Jell-O. Let it stand for 2 minutes.
4. Pour the Jell-O mixture over the cake, letting the liquid fill the holes.
5. Cover the cake and chill in the fridge for 1–2 hours.
6. Top with whipped topping and sliced strawberries.

Scan to visit

www.primaryhelper.com/downloads